SCHIRMER'S LIBRARY
OF MUSICAL CLASSICS

FRANZ WOHLFAHRT

Op. 74

Fifty Easy Melodious Studies

For the Violin

IN TWO BOOKS

Vol. 927
⟶ Book I.   First Position

Vol. 928
Book II.   Third Position

G. SCHIRMER, *Inc.*

DISTRIBUTED BY

HAL•LEONARD®
CORPORATION
7777 W. BLUEMOUND RD. P.O. BOX 13819 MILWAUKEE, WI 53213

Fifty Easy Melodious Studies

⊓ Down-bow
ᴠ Up-bow

Franz Wohlfahrt. Op. 74, Book I

Allegro moderato

1.

4

Allegro moderato

2.

Allegro moderato

3.

5

Allegro moderato

4.

Allegro moderato

5.

Allegro moderato

6.

Moderato

7.

8

Moderato assai

13.

12

Allegretto

14.

mf

Allegro con fuoco

15.

f

16. Allegro moderato

Allegro moderato

17.

Allegro

18.

Allegro moderato

19.

Allegro

20.

rit.   *a tempo*

Allegro moderato

23.

rit.

Allegro moderato

24.

rit.

a tempo